YOUTHW

Youthwork Ideas

JOHN BUCKERIDGE

KINGSWAY PUBLICATIONS
EASTBOURNE

ISBN 0 85476 440 2

Front cover design based on an original idea
by Rachel Salter. Photo: Jim Loring.

Produced by Bookprint Creative Services
P.O. Box 827, BN23 6NX, England for
KINGSWAY PUBLICATIONS LTD
Lottbridge Drove, Eastbourne, E Sussex BN23 6NT.
Printed in England by Clays Ltd, St Ives plc

To Alice: my wife, my encourager, my best friend and the source of most of my best ideas.

ACKNOWLEDGEMENTS

My thanks to John Allan, senior youth worker at Belmont Chapel, Exeter and Kevin Elliott, volunteer youth worker at Highbury Congregational Church, Cheltenham. They contributed a significant number of the ideas, which first appeared in the Ideas Factory column of *YOUTHWORK* magazine.

Contributors to the 'Love Is' chapter were: Grahame Knox, director of '2000 Years On', a Youth For Christ education initiative; Heather Evans, co-ordinator of the Capital Radiate project; and Andy Hickford, youth minister at Stopsley Baptist Church, Luton.

Thanks also to Brian Phillips and Dave Roberts who encouraged me to write this book, and to the rest of the staff at Elm House Christian Communications who put up with me on a day-to-day basis.

Thanks to staffworkers and volunteers past and present at Epping Forest Youth For Christ, particularly Bob Moffett and Tony Chapman, who gave me the opportunities to try out some of my more hair-brained ideas.

Thanks to the leaders and members of Surbiton Community Church, who released me from commitments and gave me their blessing to go and write this book.

And finally, a big thank you to my wife, Alice, who listens to my ideas and refines them, making them realistic instead of ridiculous.

CONTENTS

1. IDEAS UNLIMITED   11

   Where to look for ideas
   How to adapt youth ministry resources
   Build an ideas library

2. TRUSTBUILDERS   18

   Games and activities to build trust and friendships

3. BIBLE-ATHON   38

   Bringing the Bible to life

4. LOVE IS...   47

   Games, discussion starters and events on the theme of love, sex and relationships

5. EGGSPLORING EASTER   60

   A range of ideas to use at Easter time

6. HOT SUMMER IDEAS   71

    Outdoor games and summer socials

7. HALLOWE'EN ALTERNATIVES   88

    Making a positive response to the dark side
    of Hallowe'en

8. CHRISTMAS CRACKERS   98

    Games, fun activities and discussion starters
    to focus on the real meaning of Christmas

9. PARENTS' NIGHT   106

    A bridge-building exercise well worth doing

10. HIGH PROFILE EVENTS   115

    Four suggestions for raising the profile of
    your youth group

11. IS THERE LIFE BEYOND
    BLOXWITCH?   128

    Ideas and activities to help young people
    become aware of the needs of people from
    other countries or cultures

12. STARTS AND STOPS   140

    Ideas to help the youth group start with a
    swing—and end with a punch

13. BOOKS FOR IDEAS   149

    Over 50 youth ministry ideas books listed
    and described

I
IDEAS UNLIMITED

Whatever form of youth work you are involved in it's easy to get stuck in a rut. Instead of a varied programme that stretches and excites your young people spiritually, physically and intellectually, some youth group/club programmes resemble prime time TV on a summer evening—a series of tired old repeats!

'Variety is the spice of life' goes the saying, and young people more than most have a low boredom threshold. Most youth workers I meet in local churches and at training events, and the readers of *YOUTHWORK* magazine, all tell me that coming up with fresh programme ideas is one of their biggest problems.

My hope is that this book will be part of the solution. In the following chapters you'll find a variety of ideas to adapt and use. But the ideas here certainly aren't unlimited.

So how can you keep the fresh ideas coming?

The golden rule is to remember that there are very few truly *original* ideas. That lesson was taught to me by one of the most creative youth specialists Britain has ever produced. He taught me that with a little effort and organisation it is possible to keep variety, interest and zaniness in your youth work programme.

Where to look for ideas

There is a wide and growing range of source material which you can adapt and use in your youth programme. British and American publishers have produced a wealth of resources, from a complete through-the-year curriculum, to books and worksheets for creative Bible studies, crowdbreaker games, discussion starters and outdoor games. At the end of this book I have listed the range of ideas books available. But there is nothing like going to a well-stocked Christian bookshop and having a good browse!

I have also found the following very worthwhile sources of material which can trigger or provide good ideas: check them out.

Listening

It may seem obvious, but spending an evening socially with your young people, listening to what they are talking about, can be very educational!

It can also spark off a host of programming ideas. Preconceptions you may have about how they spend their money, or their interest (or lack of it) in a range of subjects, can be put right.

Postbox

Keep a box for ideas, suggestions and criticisms in the room where your youth group/club meet. Regularly ask members for their ideas and suggestions—tell them to write anonymously if they prefer. Get one of the young people to decorate the box. It can be made of cardboard with a flap so that members can put ideas in and you can remove and read them.

Youth TV

There is a range of television programmes particularly aimed at or popular with young people which will help keep you in touch with youth culture as well as providing a source of ideas. These include The Word, Def II, The Chart Show and The Big Breakfast.

TV game shows

Some of my wackiest games ideas have been developed from tacky game shows. When we were looking at the subject of money I adapted 'The Price Is Right' quiz show. The youngsters were invited to 'come on down' to try and guess the price of items out of catalogue books.

You could even get someone form the church who is good with models and electronics to construct a copy of a game show board. One church in the Midlands has a brilliant replica of the electronic letters board from the TV quiz 'Blockbusters'.

Teenage Magazines

Drop into your local newsagents at least once a month and buy a couple of teenage magazines, eg *Just Seventeen, Smash Hits, Sky, Mizz, iD*.

I get some great ideas from reading these magazines, as well as staying in touch with what some of my youth group read.

Once I cut out some of the questions published in an agony aunt column and asked our youth group to come up with their solution to the problems. The resulting discussion was both revealing and a lot of fun as we chatted together and considered what the Bible said on the issues raised.

The only drawback to buying teenage magazines is the funny looks you get from behind the counter when you pay for your copy of *Jackie* or *My Guy*—especially if you are a bloke!

Ideas Swopshop

Organise a town-wide Ideas Swopshop for youth leaders/workers. You could ask everyone to bring one good idea which they have used in their youth programme recently to share with others. Everyone should then go away with some good ideas as well as having had the chance to make new friends and useful contacts. Make sure you schedule some prayer time together.

BBC Radio 5

The evening programmes are often youth oriented and worth checking out.

Newspapers

Daily papers, especially tabloids, contain plenty of human interest stories which you can use in a variety of ways in your programme. A story about a model who apparently has everything—but kills herself, or the trial of a teenage joyrider who badly hurt a pedestrian, will provide you with a starting point to get your young people talking. From basic good-versus-evil, right and wrong type stories to 'grey' issues of morality or ethics— newspapers provide rich pickings for talks, worksheets or discussion starters.

Conferences

Attending a good youth leaders' conference like Brainstormers for a day or weekend will provide you with a hatful of new ideas, as well as encouraging and stimulating your thinking. Informal contacts made during coffee and meal breaks, where you can share problems and ideas, are often almost as valuable as the seminars and workshops.

YOUTHWORK magazine

Each issue of *YOUTHWORK* magazine is stuffed full of fresh ideas. From discussion starters to games, ready-to-use meeting outlines to evangelism ideas—it's got the lot. Available from your local Christian bookshop or by subscription—for details write to: *YOUTHWORK*, 37 Elm Road, New Malden, Surrey KT3 3HB, or telephone 081-942 9761 during office hours.

How to adapt youth ministry resources

When coming up with a week-by-week programme it is tempting to swallow a whole resource from a book, scheme, video, complete meeting guide or whatever. But this tends to result in a stilted ill-fitting programme which fails to take into account the uniqueness of your youth group.

You need to personalise the material to take into account your gifting and ability and the needs of your group. This could mean dropping certain suggested activities, changing the material to relate to your local culture, or linking in to some topical piece of news to make the material more relevant or alive to your young people.

One other mistake to avoid is to presume you know where your young people are at on any given subject. A little research beforehand can help you pitch the evening at their level, taking them on in their knowledge, experience, maturity and understanding, instead of going over old ground, or—just as bad—pitching things three steps ahead of where they are.

If you ignore this simple precaution your presumptions about your youth group's understanding and/or experience of a subject could be wide of the mark. You could end up talking way over their heads or leave them feeling they have been treated like little kids if you miscalculate and fail to do any research.

Talk with your young people, ask them to fill out mini-questionnaires or worksheets, or in a group discussion ask questions which aim to uncover what they already know on the subject. It will be time well spent and you could learn a thing or two which will suprise you!

Build an ideas library

The ideas are out there, we bump into them every day, but if you fail to write them down, tear out the cutting, video the programme or whatever, they are just as quickly lost again. That is why it is helpful to build yourself an ideas library.

One well-known British evangelist catalogues cuttings and other ideas and then keeps them in a collection of shoe boxes. One of the things that marks him out is his regular and original use of good illustrations when he preaches.

A little organisation frees you from the tyranny of a blank page and an empty mind when you desperately need an idea for a game, an illustration for a talk, or a worksheet outline.

2
TRUSTBUILDERS

Many youth clubs/groups have a summer break. This factor, combined with the arrival of newcomers who have graduated from younger church-based groups during the first weeks back after the break, make it vital that you include some trust-building activities. These help to overcome initial shyness and awkwardness, and encourage co-operation and the formation of new friendships.

During the first few weeks of the new programme it is important to help the process of integration and minimalise the formation of cliques. Expecting young people to take the initiative is unrealistic. The following ideas will provide opportunities for the group to gel and get established.

However, don't forget that what works with one group of young people can die a death elsewhere. Never be afraid to adapt ideas for your young people.

One very important principle to bear in mind: games, crowdbreakers, discussion starters, etc, should never belittle or embarrass anyone.

GETTING TO KNOW YOU

This guessing game helps to introduce people to each other in a fun way. Divide the group into fours and fives. Members then take it in turns to choose a category from those listed below. He or she reads the first question aloud to the rest of the group and they have to guess what the answer is most likely to be. All who guess right collect a point. One person in each group keeps the score. Make sure that everyone gets two goes to choose from the available categories.

The winner in each group is the person who collects the most points.

Fashion

1. I am more likely to shop at:
   (a) Top Shop
   (b) Burton or Dorothy Perkins

2. When I buy clothes I look for:
   (a) brand name
   (b) price

3. When I buy clothes I usually:
   (a) shop all day
   (b) buy the first thing I try on

4. My favourite colour in clothes is:
   (a) blue
   (b) black

(c) red
(d) green
(e) another colour

Food

1. I would prefer a meal in:
   (a) Pizza Hut
   (b) posh restaurant

2. When it comes to cooking food:
   (a) I am a good cook
   (b) I am hopeless at cooking

3. I would rather eat:
   (a) fish and chips
   (b) lasagne

4. My favourite way of eating eggs is:
   (a) fried
   (b) boiled
   (c) scrambled
   (d) poached
   (e) I don't like egg

School

1. I would prefer to go to:
   (a) mixed sex school
   (b) single sex school

2. My attitude towards teachers is:
   (a) they're okay

(b) they don't like me, and I don't like them

3. My attendance level at school is:
   (a) less than five days off sick during a year
   (b) a week or more off sick in the past year

4. My best subject at school is:
   (a) English
   (b) maths
   (c) PE
   (d) art
   (e) something else

Cars

1. If I had a car it would be:
   (a) spotless
   (b) grubby

2. If I had a car I would prefer it to be:
   (a) my choice of colour
   (b) fast

3. If I become a driver I am likely to be:
   (a) a careful driver
   (b) a reckless driver

4. The car that would suit me best would be:
   (a) vintage Rolls Royce
   (b) Herbie-style Volkswagen
   (c) turbo-charged Ferrari
   (d) Knight Rider

(e) old Ford Cortina with fluffy dice hanging from the mirror.

Travel

1. When it comes to holidays I prefer:
   (a) sun and beaches
   (b) activity holidays

2. If I had £200 to spend I would choose:
   (a) one luxurious night in a 5-star hotel
   (b) 7-day cheap package holiday

3. When I go on a trip I:
   (a) travel light
   (b) take the kitchen sink

4. My ideal holiday destination would be:
   (a) Australia
   (b) Israel
   (c) Florida
   (d) Butlins at Bognor
   (e) Kenya

CHE-E-E-E-SE

A new group photo to put onto your noticeboard will focus everyone's attention on the fact that the group includes several newcomers. But don't go for a standard boring photo. Try one of these wacky ideas for a zany group picture.

High jump

On the count of three everyone, except the cameraman jumps. You'll need fast film in the camera to get a good picture.

Head shot

Climb a ladder, tree or lean out of a second storey window and get everyone to look up at you for a photograph with a difference.

Jaques Cousteau

Buy or borrow an all-weather camera and take your youth club/group to a swimming pool. Get them in the shallow end, tell them to take a deep breath and duck. You duck too, focus and shoot underwater. The resulting photograph should look great.

BRIDGE-BUILDER

Divide the group into teams of three or four in such a way that groups are thoroughly mixed as regards age, gender, cliques.

Provide each group with an equal amount of bridge-building materials, eg, card, pipecleaners, safety pins, sellotape, glue and have available material for decorating—felt-tip pens, transfers, etc. Specify the size of the ravine to be spanned, eg 40cm, and give them the width of the 'heavy die-cast' car which must cross the bridge. Tell them that the bottom of the ravine (gap between two tables) is a shark-infested foaming river (a bucket of gunge), from which they must recover their vehicle if the whole bridge fails.

Allocate a certain amount of time for planning, then ample time for construction, after which you test each bridge by pushing the car along it, while all the groups watch. You could tie group members' left hands together before asking them to recover the car from the gunge—with the joint hand.

Complete the exercise by adding equal weights to the surviving bridges, until only one is left. Offer prizes for the strongest bridge and the best-looking one!

TRUE OR FALSE

Each week ask one young person to prepare ten facts about themselves or their family which you write on a chalkboard or overhead projector before the meeting. Some of the facts should be true, others invented. At the beginning of the meeting introduce the participant (encouraging rapturous applause), who then reads out each statement for the group to ponder on.

At the end of the evening, the participant comes to the front again, and by a show of hands on each statement the group votes on which they think are true and which false. If the majority of the group vote 'true' and the statement is false, the participant gets a point, if the group guesses correctly the group gets a point.

Be sure to give lots of encouragement to all who take a turn, especially if they score low. Don't forget the objective is to enable the group to know each other better, and to encourage group participation.

SILHOUETTES

Have ready some black paper cut into A5 sheets. Divide the group into pairs who do not know each other well. Give out paper and scissors to everyone. The object is to cut out a head-and-shoulders silhouette of your partner and to find out five important facts about them, eg, hobby, favourite sport, film, etc. Allow time to complete the task, then go into presentation time. Each pair will go up to the front of the group. No 1 will place the cut-out of her partner directly onto your OHP plate, giving partner's name and facts. No 2 then does the same, so that both silhouettes are showing together. Then move to the next pair. The silhouettes will often look strange and cause a lot of laughter, but the exercise will help the groups get to know each other. It adds interest if you can find an artist to give a good demonstration first. At the end you could mount all the silhouettes on white card, and write names underneath, for display.

WAR ZONE

Divide the group into small units of four to six, and explain that they are war casualties and each unit must get their members back to base. Set up an obstacle course, perhaps using two or three rooms of your building, where they have to pick up supplies (eg Chewits, M&Ms, etc). Assign disabilities to the units, ie each No 1 has no sight (blindfold) and cannot talk; each No 2 cannot walk; each No 3 has a broken arm, etc. A good balance is required so that the exercise is possible, but that they need to co-operate well to succeed. Announce that the teams who do not cheat can eat their supplies when back at base.

You can enhance this game by using face paints and medical supplies (bandages, crutches, etc) to make up the casualties before commencing, and by playing a tape of battle sound effects in the background. Carefully supervise the game to make sure that no-one actually gets injured!

RECORDBREAKERS

Ask members of the group to bring along an old LP record from their collection that they would rather not admit to owning. Perhaps they could take one of their parents horror-records (with their permission). You'll find all sorts of nasties will turn up, like Donny Osmond, Bros, Bay City Rollers, Wham, etc. Each person introduces himself and his record while everyone else makes suitable groaning noises. Use the records to build attendance levels: 'Next week we'll smash this awful Bros album if we can beat this weeks' attendance of eighteen. Please try and bring a friend so we can do the world a favour and get rid of this record!'

Next week if nineteen or more attend hang the record on a piece of string and invite someone to smash it with a hammer (be careful of sharp pieces). Really build up the record-breaking big time.

Then bring out the next horror album and announce the new target to beat before it can be broken.

Another variation of this game is to go to a large field or park and have a competition to see who can throw their record the furthest. Frame the winning record and hang it up in your meeting room. Give a record token to the winner thrower.

KICK OFF

A great game for a warm autumn evening. Get everyone to line up then loosen their shoes or trainers. On the word 'go' everyone kicks off their right shoe, aiming to get it the furthest. Then on the second command 'go' it's off with the left shoe. Award a pair of odour eaters or talcum powder for the person who kicked their shoes the furthest.

Probably the funniest part of this game is retrieving shoes from the pile afterwards.

TOUCHY

Ask for a volunteer who stands in the middle of the room. Then tell everyone else they must touch some part of his or her arm or leg. You will be amazed just how many people can achieve this—the record currently stands at 26.

It certainly helps to break down some barriers, as you can't help but be a bit friendlier to someone who has been breathing in your ear and crushing your arm!

STRAWBERRY NOSE

Apply a generous blob of jam to everyone's nose. Then divide the group into two teams formed into lines. The object of the game is to pass a cotton wool ball down the line by passing it from nose to nose. The cotton wool gets pretty jammy by the end of the line!

Be sure to take photos or video this game to show later.

ALPHABETTI

Buy ten or more tins of alphabet spaghetti and empty them into one very large bowl. Put people into teams of two, make sure that the newcomers get mixed up well with more established group/club members. Then call out simple questions that have three-letter answers such as what is the minister's Christian name? Answer—Bob.

The youngsters have to dig their hands into the bowl to find the appropriate letters to make up the word which is the answer. The first team to present the answer with the letters lined up correctly on a plate or piece of kitchen paper gets a point.

Make sure you cover the floor with newspaper or plastic sheeting as this is a mega-messy game—but lots of fun.

Announce at the end of the game that as a special treat tonight you will be serving up spaghetti on toast for everyone!

MYSTERY STAR PROFILE

Use a list of standard questions based on the format used in teen mags for popstars or sportsmen/women, eg favourite meal/colour/TV programme; my most frightening moment; I would like to be on a desert island with..., etc.

You could have a photocopied set of these questions to give out at the end of a meeting for next week's 'star' to take home and fill out. Alternatively everyone could complete a form one week and hand it in for use on future weeks. The aim is for members of the group to guess who the 'star' member is from the answers provided.

WHO IS THE HERO?

Sit in a circle (maximum 15) and send one person (the sleuth) out of the room wearing a detective-type overcoat, Sherlock Holmes hat or something similar. Choose one other person to be the 'hero'. The sleuth returns, and stands in the middle of the circle where he or she must find out who the hero is. The sleuth may ask five questions, to which the group can shout back the answer. Eg, has the hero got dark hair? Does the hero go to Grimly High?

The competitive element is to see how few questions are needed to guess correctly. An incorrect guess as to the identity of the hero counts as two questions. Once the hero is revealed he or she puts on the props, becomes the sleuth, and the game continues.

BODY SCULPTURE

Divide the group into teams of about five people. Read out a shape or an object which the team must make as a group. Start with easy ones done on the floor, eg heart, letter 'S', then ask for shapes that require more co-operation and contact, eg pyramid, overhead projector. Finally ask for some living sculptures, (watching for creative movement) eg erupting volcano, Roman chariot. This activity requires a high degree of interaction, touching and co-operation.

CLAUSTROPHOBIA

Find a large empty cupboard, small room or closet and, with teams taking it in turns, see how many members they can get into it—and close the door. Simple but fun. An alternative is to have one member blindfold his team-mates, and then see how many he can get in. Beware of people getting hurt or trampled.

BOILER BULGE

This is a relay race where each team has an old baggy boiler suit and a dozen blown-up balloons. When the whistle blows, the first runner puts on the boiler suit, team-mates shove all the balloons into it, he or she runs around a marker, then returns. The team helps get the balloons out, then the next runner puts on the boiler suit, and so on. Have spare balloons ready to replace burst ones.

3
BIBLE-ATHON

Teaching the Bible, encouraging the young people you work with to explore the scriptures, should be very high on the list of your priorities. But all too often, while we spend time, energy and money to ensure other parts of our programme are creative and exciting, our Bible study remains in the Dark Ages.

So read on for some fresh methods to help your youth group discover age-old truths. I believe that it can be a realistic goal to expect street-wise kids to get excited about scripture!

SWEDISH BIBLE STUDY

Useful in an emergency, the Swedish method is particularly applicable for use with parables, psalms and sections of the epistles.

Hand out 10cm by 15cm cards with five symbols on the left side. After reading through the Bible passage, each person writes on the card next to the appropriate symbol (top to bottom): what the passage says about God; about human nature; a new insight; something which is unclear or a question which arises out of the text; a command or action to obey. Share findings in a general discussion.

BIBLE TIME WARP

Use a Bible story (eg from the Gospels) and assign everyone in the group to play the role of one of the characters. If you have more young people than characters either they double up, so two people take on one character, or get the rest to play the part of the crowd.

Ask everyone to close their eyes while you read the story aloud. Ask them to concentrate on thinking how their character feels as the story unfolds. You can either pause during the story or wait until the conclusion before asking each character in turn to describe their feelings of anger, surprise, thankfulness, etc. Encourage interaction between characters in role.

LOCATION BIBLE STUDIES

Make the Bible come alive by reading and studying stories in their original context, eg Jesus calms
the storm (Luke 8) read in a rowing boat(s) on a
lake or swimming pool; God's power to create the
stars (Psalm 8) during a midnight picnic. This
requires considerable forward planning and
depends on site availability, but will certainly
make the study memorable.

FILL IN THE BLANKS

Choose a Bible passage from the epistles which teaches an important Christian doctrine, or select a story which your group is unlikely to know about. Write the story out on a worksheet, blackboard or OHP, but leave some words blank. Working as individuals or in small groups they decide what words they think are appropriate to fill in the blanks.

Read out their answers, then read out the original scripture version; compare the differences and talk about why Jesus or the biblical author chose the words they did.

SWORD DRILL

This golden oldie game is great for improving knowledge about the order and location of Bible books.

Ensure everyone has a copy of the Bible which you refer to as the 'sword'. The game begins with everyone's sword in their sheath (Bibles under arms). On the command 'draw your swords' Bibles are held aloft while you then read out a book chapter and verse. On the command 'go' the hunt begins. The first person to start reading out the correct verse is the winner.

If you want to be really nasty call out Hezekiah chapter three verse one. Be prepared to protect yourself from flying Bibles when you admit there is no such book in the Bible as Hezekiah!

WORD ASSOCIATION

This exercise helps young people think more deeply about a Bible character or a theological or ethical concept.

Hand out worksheets like the one below. In the centre ask the group to write in the key word (name of person or concept) which relates to the theme of the meeting. The young people then fill in the boxes around the key word with descriptive words. Tell them to write in the word that first occurs to them. Assure them that they can write in what they want—not what they think you expect or want—be open and honest.

When everyone has completed the exercise discuss the words they chose. This should result in a better understanding of a biblical character or concept, learned in a non-threatening style.

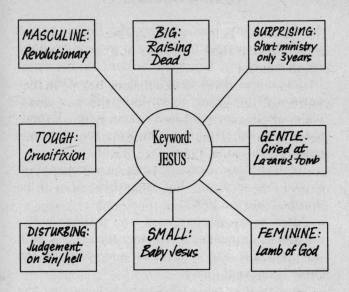

MASCULINE:
Revolutionary

BIG:
Raising
Dead

SURPRISING:
Short ministry
only 3 years

TOUGH:
Crucifixion

Keyword:
JESUS

GENTLE.
Cried at
Lazarus tomb

DISTURBING:
Judgement
on sin/hell

SMALL:
Baby Jesus

FEMININE:
Lamb of God

PARAPHRASE

Choose a short passage from the Bible and ask your young people to rewrite it as though it had happened today. If it is an incident, eg the arrest of Jesus, ask them to write it in the style of a newspaper, including a punchy headline. A parable could be rewritten as a drama script. Experiment with other parts of scripture too—eg as a psalm rewritten as a rap!

Explain that the central truth or teaching point should be retained, but everything should be updated into the 1990s.

After everyone has read out their re-writes encourage discussion on whether the central truth was retained and explained, and whether the Bible is relevant today.

Explain that most Christians believe that the Bible is inspired by God but that the individuals who wrote it expressed their own personalities and writing styles. You only have to compare the Gospels to see that.

The Door magazine in its May/June 1993 issue asked how different would the Bible be if it were to be inspired and written today by twentieth century authors. What do your young people think?

4
LOVE IS...

Here is a selection of games, discussion starters and a social event for you to adapt and use on Valentine's Day, or when you next look at the subject of love, sex or relationships.

Valentine's Day is a special day for many teenagers. Some will be tentatively expressing affection for someone for the first time by sending them a valentine card. However it is also a time of depression for many who don't get cards, who may feel ugly or failures because they don't have a girl or boyfriend. Why not use Valentine's Day as an opportunity for young people to discover what the Bible talks about as *real* love, rather than lust or an obsession?

LOVE IS...

Provide your group with a very large sheet of card or a noticeboard with the words 'Love Is...' at the top. Supply them with a pile of magazines and newspapers, plenty of felt-tip pens, glue, scissors and A4 sheets of paper. They have thirty minutes to work together on a collage to illustrate the theme.

When the time is up, get the young people to talk you through their picture highlighting different opinions and images of what love is.

Conclude by reading out 1 Corinthians 13:4-7. Discuss the similarities and differences between scripture and their picture.

EXPRESSIONS OF LOVE

Ask for two couples to volunteer. Then explain they will need to face their partner and share their deepest feelings of love for each other! Phrases which they repeat are held up behind their partner by a helper. They must repeat each phrase with as much feeling and sincerity as possible. The phrases alternate between the boy and girl. The only catch is that each person has a bag of marshmallows which they feed their partner one at a time, before each line.

Chewing or swallowing the marshmallows is not allowed. The first couple to fail to express their next line due to uncontrollable laughter or an inability to speak loses.

Lots of cheering and clapping should be encouraged. Give an appropriate prize for the winning couple: tubes of 'Love Hearts' sherbert sweets or Rolos ('Do you love someone enough to give them your last Rolo?'). For the losing couple a consolation prize of a packet of marshmallows could be appropriate!

Suggested phrases:
Boy: You are so beautiful
Girl: You are so strong
Boy: I love the way you laugh
Girl: You are so rugged and handsome
Boy: I love you, my darling
Girl: I will love you for ever

Boy: My love for you knows no bounds
Girl: My heart is filled with love for you
Boy: Your smile makes me go weak at the knees
Girl: You are the most wonderful boy in the universe

etc...

TILL DEATH US DO PART

Invite a widow or widower in your church family to come to the youth club to be interviewed. Obviously choose the person with care and sensitivity. Ask them questions about their partner and encourage them to show photographs of their loved one. Try to focus on how God's love has sustained them through their loss.

THE LOVE TRACK

Tape a montage of love song snippets currently in, or recently in, the charts. Play back the clips—the young people need to identify each song title and artist.

An alternative is to collect recent copies of *Smash Hits* magazine and write on an OHP acetate sheet short parts from the lyrics from recent love songs, printed in the magazine.

Apart from being fun, this game can be used to emphasise the obsession of pop music with the subject of love.

KARAOKE CLUB

A cheap and easy alternative to the full-blown karaoke is to buy one of the karaoke cassettes generally available in record stores and do it yourself. Set up a small PA system with two or three microphones and get volunteers to sing along to some classic love songs with a karaoke tape or record.

Most high street record stores will have a range of karaoke albums for sale. The lyrics are normally sold with the album. To get the evening off to a good start you may need to offer to sing the first song yourself!

Applaud all performers heartily, even if they sing some flat notes, and encourage people to sing in pairs or in threesomes, with the audience joining in the chorus and clapping along, to make the karaoke go with a swing.

LOVE IS BLIND

Ask for a girl and a boy to volunteer—explain that each is to get their partner ready for a date. Ask them to face each other, place a towel round their shoulders and blindfold them both. Give each a bag and explain that it contains all the items necessary to get their partner ready. They can take out an object at a time and apply it to their partners face. Good fun and very messy!

The girl's bag should contain: shaving cream, razor (blade removed!), comb. The boy's bag should contain: lipstick, hairbrush, toothpaste and brush.

THE DATING GAME

Give each person a role card which tells them their name, age, job, hobbies, likes and dislikes, ideal dream person of the opposite sex, family background, and religious views. Then let them mingle, chat to one another, and find the person who they believe is the right partner for them. They only have two minutes for each conversation before moving on (although if they find someone totally unsuitable they can move on quicker).

Just as in real life you don't get to meet all the possible partners there are, so in this game each person will probably have time to speak with only five or six others.

When a fair number have found partners (it doesn't have to be everybody—real life is like that), stop the game and analyse the results.

Why did some people feel they had found the right person? Why did others reject each other? Do opposites attract, or is similarity of interests more important? Which are the most important qualities to take into account? Did the cards omit information you'd like to have had? How does all this tie up with biblical guidelines on relationships and marriage?

WHAT IS LOVE?

Divide into groups of three or four. Each group needs a Bible, paper and pen. Give each group one of the following Bible passages to read and report back on. They need to answer the following questions:

1. How would you describe Jesus' actions and words, eg mushy, sentimental, warm?

2. Was Jesus responding to what people needed or what people deserved? Does this tell us anything about God's love for us?

3. 'True love involves action'—discuss.

4. What practical ways can we love people 'the Jesus way'?

Passages to read: Luke 23:32-43; John 4:1-38; John 8:1-11; John 11:1-44; John 18:15-27; John 21:15-19.

Whether or not you got a Valentine's card,
you are invited to:
**A FONDUE—BECAUSE WE'RE FOND OF
YOU!**

A fondue evening is a lot of fun and can be organised without too much work or hassle. You will need one fondue set for about every eight people, or if you can't get hold of a fondue set, use large saucepans and ordinary forks.

A fondue can be as simple or as posh as you like. You may choose to serve a variety of different meats and sauces with salads or side dishes, or simply cook a massive cheese sauce and serve it with chunks of french bread. Another variation is a chocolate fondue, with chunks of madeira cake, marshmallows or fruit to dip.

If your group is very large, why not serve the food on a big board on the floor, with everyone sitting round? If you have several different dishes give them romantic names such as: Cheese Cherish; Peach Passion; Venus Punch; Chocolate Devotion—or use a thesaurus and make up your own names!

If someone loses the food from their fork in the pot, they have to do a forfeit—have some appropriate ones planned. Add to the atmosphere by making the occasion candlelit. If possible have a small lamp that can be used as a spotlight for anyone undergoing a forfeit.

Forfeit question ideas:

1. What cuddly toys have you got? Go on, own up!
2. Who was your first love?
3. What is your favourite sloppy record?
4. What food do you love?
5. Complete these couples from the Bible: Adam and ?; Ruth and ?; Abraham and ?; Samson and ?; Mary and ?.
6. Complete these famous cartoon couples: Popeye and ?; Fred Flintstone and ?; Mickey Mouse and ?.

Answers (if you weren't sure):
5. Eve, Boaz, Sarah, Delilah, Joseph.
6. Olive, Wilma, Minnie.

PARTNERS

Give each person a slip of paper with one half of a
well-known pair of friends. Tell them they have to
find their partners by miming their part. They
cannot talk (apart from guessing an identity), or
show anyone their piece of paper.

Suggestions for pairs:
Laurel and Hardy; Robin Hood and Maid Mar-
ion; Bill and Ben (flowerpot men); Torvill and
Dean; Lone Ranger and Tonto; Punch and Judy;
Darth Vader and Luke Skywalker; Postman Pat
and Jess the cat.

5
EGGSPLORING EASTER

In the Early Church, new converts were baptised on Easter Sunday morning, after an all-night vigil. How about locking yourselves into the church building from 10pm on Saturday through to Easter Sunday morning?

The programme doesn't need to be all serious—it can include games, videos, snacks at unearthly hours, etc—but it could be a useful learning and worshipping experience centred on Easter, perhaps including some of the other ideas below. End the night with a sunrise service outside somewhere, and a big breakfast.

Plan the programme with care. Include a few surprise items to wake people up just when they are starting to get tired. If you feel that staying awake all night is too challenging, why not give them three hours' sleep in shifts—so that someone is always awake.

PASCHAL CONTROVERSY

Sadly Easter has caused lots of disagreements in the Christian church, mainly over when it should be! Ask the group if they know what Quartodecimanism is. (They won't!) It's the belief that Easter should fall on the fourteenth day of the Jewish month Nisan, and not the next convenient Sunday—and believe it or not, it caused raised voices and hard feelings at one stage of church history.

Get small groups to invent a new 'paschal controversy' over something really insignificant which could get Christians arguing! How about the precise theological significance of Easter eggs, or the number of hot cross buns which a truly spiritual Christian should be allowed to consume in one sitting? Then argue about it.

Use the exercise as a launch into a discussion about why Christians argue, and how vital it is to focus on the big things that unite us rather than the tiny points which can cause dissension. Stress the big things about Easter on which all Christians are agreed. Perhaps use Philippians 1:27-2:4 as a scripture base.

EGGSPLORING EGGS

Easter eggs have little to do with the Christian meaning of Easter. Or do they? First test your group's knowledge of Easter Egg trivia with a 'true or false' quiz:

1. The Romans placed eggs in graves. (T)
2. Jews in Galicia used to eat an egg for luck when they came home from a party. (F—it was when they came home from a funeral).
3. In 1979 David S. Donoghue got himself into the *Guinness Book of Records* by dropping fresh eggs 650ft from a helicopter onto a Tokyo golf course. They didn't break. (T)
4. In 1989 in Finland Risto Antikainen threw an egg 318ft. His friend Jryki Korhonen, caught it. The shell was only slightly cracked. (F—it was completely unbroken).
5. The heaviest chicken's egg ever laid was produced by a Rhode Island Red chicken belonging to a farmer in Hampshire. On the 21st January 1956, the champion chicken laid a monster egg which contained nine yokes and weighed an incredible 2lb 1oz. (F—you must be yoking!).
6. There's a cathedral in Singapore covered in a plaster which hasn't needed replacing for over a hundred years—it's so tough and durable. It was made out of egg whites. (T)

7. British hens produce 12,500 dozen eggs every hour. (F—it's 125,000 dozen).

Use all this to say: eggs are very common little objects, but people have made a lot of fuss about them throughout history. In the eighteenth century, a French bridegroom, instead of carrying his new wife over the threshold, would break an egg there, as a sign that he hoped she would have lots of babies.

Why the fuss about eggs?

1. *Eggs are a promise of new life.*
2. *Eggs have remarkable properties*—they're the perfect shape to protect the emerging life inside, and they contain everything inside them that the new life needs. Many baby animals who grow inside eggs are born with a special 'egg tooth' so that they can chip their way out when the time is right.
3. *Eggs have to be broken before the life can emerge.*

Use these three points as the basis for a talk or Bible study based on say, John 12:23-36, about the meaning of Easter.

EGG BLOW

An oldie but goodie. Get a 2ft length of ½″ diameter clear plastic tubing and crack an egg into it. Then stand one volunteer at either end blowing hard...

RAISING DOUGH

Use Easter as a time to raise money for missions or relief work. Take orders for traditional Easter eggs of the sort nobody makes any more—boiled in coloured dye for a long time (so that they'll keep for years), with a personal design or message scratched on them first by the artistic people in your group.

Or bake monster hot cross buns—same recipe as usual, but in a 7in. cake tin!

As we all know, Easter is about the death and resurrection of Jesus. But so many other things have been mixed up with it—fluffy chicks, eggs, bunnies—that you could be excused for thinking it has nothing to do with Christianity.

Divide your group into teams and give them the job of devising a completely spurious account of how Easter came about—and then present it in dramatic form to the rest of the group. It must include Easter eggs, hot cross buns, Simnel cake, the Easter bunny, and the seasonal opening of stately homes. It must not include any reference to Jesus or the Christian faith.

Give cream eggs to the team with the best account. Use the activity to get them thinking about the real meaning of Easter—and how it loses all coherence if you leave out the cross and the empty tomb.

LOCAL HOLY LAND TOUR

Ask your group to think through the events of the Easter story. Suppose it had all happened in your town...where would it have happened?

Send them out to find 'Gethsemane' (the local park?), the judgement hall (magistrates court?), Golgotha (the rubbish dump?), the empty tomb (the cemetery?). Give them extra clues if necessary (if, for instance, there's more than one possible park or graveyard).

Station someone at all the points so that each group arriving at the correct location can be given something to prove they were there. For example, a 'soldier' guarding the tomb could give them a feather from his helmet. A servant girl outside the magistrates court could give them a charred stick from the fire where Peter warmed himself.

The first group back with a full collection of items wins a large chocolate egg.

Used properly, this kind of treasure hunt can be a great medium for reinforcing knowledge of the events of Jesus' trial, death and resurrection. Don't tell them everything—make them use the bits of knowledge they already possess.

THE RESURRECTION GAME

Did the resurrection happen? Christians are good at supplying evidence to demolish any other theory about what happened to Jesus' body. But normally we do it in a straight talk. How about turning the resurrection evidence into a game which allows people to pick up the facts as they participate?

Divide into small groups. Give each group a sheet of paper which lists the main alternative theories:

- Jesus didn't die, but escaped.
- The disciples or grave-robbers stole the body.
- The Romans or Jews removed the body.
- The story is just an exaggerated legend.

Then send them around to gather as much evidence as they can to disprove any of these theories. You could have some facts—eg about Jesus' wounds, the guard around the tomb, the 'blood and water'—written out on pieces of paper attached to the wall. You could have a cassette report for groups to swich on and listen to, about, say, the way in which Jewish bodies were prepared for burial, or what Jewish grave-robbers used to look for when they robbed a tomb. There are plenty of facts available in books such as Josh McDowell's *Evidence That Demands A Verdict* (Scripture Press) or Michael Green's *You Must Be*

Joking (Hodder). You could even leave some of those books lying about, perhaps with markers in certain pages. While the game is in progress, you could go round placing extra clues, perhaps with some helpful verses.

Make the game more interesting by introducing a trading element; give each group some but not all of the facts, so they have to trade information with one another to build up the complete picture. If you give them some bits which are meaningless, and other bits which are important, they will have to work out carefully the value of what they are trading.

When we played this, we increased the competitiveness by locking a large bar of chocolate into a case with a combination lock. When groups thought they had enough information to disprove one of the theories, they would come to me, and if I agreed, I would give them one of the four combination numbers. The first group to get all four numbers were able to open the case and claim the chocolate.

EGGSENTRIC IDEAS

Human beings have found a lot of different things to do with eggs at Easter time: egg rolling, jumping, tapping, hunting. There is a man in the Midlands who specialises in jumping on eggs with both feet, then jumping off again immediately, without breaking the eggs.

You may not want to do this one—it can get a little messy!—but how about issuing small groups with an egg or two each and challenging them to come up with a completely new idea for a sport or pastime involving eggs?

Note: in order to save getting egg yolk all over the floor, and also so as not to waste valuable food, why not empty out the eggs first by pricking a hole in each end, blowing out the contents into a cup, refilling with water and re-sealing the egg with a dab of wax or a sticky label?

6
HOT SUMMER IDEAS

Here's a selection of hot games ideas to use with your youth group/club outdoors on warm summer nights.

GUESS THE GARGLE

Divide the group into teams and hand each person a cup of water. The teams take it in turns to gargle their way through a tune which the other teams attempt to guess.

For 'churched' youngsters you could have a 'name that chorus' competition.

To turn giggles into laughter substitute water with lemonade. The bubbles make gargling a ticklish business.

Make sure you have plenty of paper towels handy.

Award bottles of mouthwash to the winning team.

LATE NIGHT VOLLEYBALL

Buy a light-stick (available from most joke and novelty shops) and put it inside a large balloon which is then inflated. Put down some fluorescent tape as court markings and play by the usual volleyball rules. If you play this indoors, turn out the lights. As an alternative to the balloon you could spray a beach ball with fluorescent paint.

TAPE BALL

Here's a variation of basketball or netball that prevents the best players from dominating the game.

Divide the group into two teams. Every time someone scores put a plastic sandwich bag over one of their hands, get them to make a fist, then tape up their hand. If the same person scores again tape up their other hand. This handicaps the best players and gets more people into the game.

Use Scotch tape or parcel tape and ensure you tape over the bag, not bare skin, as this can cause an allergic rash on some people.

BLANKET RACES

To play this game you need some old blankets and a grassy area. Divide the group into teams of four. One member sits on a corner of the blanket and grips the edges tightly, while the other three haul him along using the front edge of the blanket. It's fast, furious and very tiring!

Variations include: 'Grand Prix'—a circular track where the race is a given number of laps; 'Hill Start'—teams in pairs or singly pull up a steep grassy hill against the clock; 'Blanket Relay' in lanes—the pulling team swaps partners in relay style.

ROUND-UP

This group game works best in a wooded area. Divide the young people into teams of equal numbers, ideally between five and eight. Team members are linked together with a rope which is loosely tied round each person's waist. Each group has a three minute start on the catchers (two individuals). The groups must escape capture (achieved when one of the group is tagged) by moving quickly and quietly together. This game requires co-operative behaviour as the teams must work together as a unit. You could follow this game up with a discussion on working together and co-operation.

Safety notes: give groups clear instructions on the boundaries to prevent teams getting hopelessly lost. Ensure rope is loosely tied over clothing around the waist to prevent rope-burn or worse.

FROSTBITE

What a way to cool off on a hot summer day!

Volunteers sit on a low stool, take shoes and socks off and, using their toes, lift marbles out of washing-up bowls. The sting in the tail is that as well as a dozen marbles you pour in a pile of ice cubes (you'll need lots). The first to remove all the marbles from their bowl is the winner. Give an ice-pole as a prize.

A fun variation is to use spaghetti with tomato sauce instead of ice.

AUSSIE CHRISTMAS

Have you ever celebrated Christmas in August? You could develop a whole weekend away—a camp or houseparty around the theme of the Incarnation—based on this idea.

Cook and eat a Christmas meal with all the trimmings. Decorate the room with tinsel, a plastic tree with lights, etc. Have some Christmassy music playing in the background. Play some traditional Christmas party games, sing carols, do an alternative Queen's speech, hand out Christmas cards, etc.

Make the point that the Christian festival of Christmas was superimposed onto a pagan celebration and that no one knows the exact date when Christ was born. So celebrating Christmas in August is just as valid as on 25th December.

JUNK FOOD CRAWL

Here is the ultimate greasy-fast-food-athon. Check out the local fast-food options and prepare a menu beforehand (with prices) to give your group an appetite, and ask them to come prepared with adequate funds. It needn't cost the earth as portions can be shared and you can negotiate a reduced group-rate.

Here is a sample menu:

St Desmond's Youth Club
Junk Food Crawl

MENU

Hors d'Oeuvres: French Fries
at McDonalds
Entree: Pizza at Pizza Hut
Dessert: Cheesecake at
Kentucky Fried Chicken
Tea / coffee / soft drink:
Joe's Roadside Cafe

BUBBLEMANIA

You'll need two identical children's paddling pools, a large bottle of bubble bath and access to a hosepipe for this wet, wet game.

Fill both paddling pools half full with cold water and then pour in equal quantities of bubble bath.

Two teams are each allocated a paddling pool. The winning team is the first to stir up enough bubbly foam to come above the level of the top of the pool.

Your young people will never have cleaner hands than after this game!

TASTEBUD CONFUSION

Can your youngsters tell the difference between Coke and Pepsi? Find out with this soft-drink taste-test.

Arrange drinks in glasses labelled A, B, C, etc. Keep a careful note of what drink goes into what glass. Obviously this needs to be done out of sight.

Suggested soft drinks to use are: Coke, Pepsi, Diet Coke, 7-Up, Lemonade, Lilt, Fanta, Sunkist, Tizer, Irn-Bru.

ROBBERS AND INDIANS

When we were little we played cops and robbers and cowboys and Indians. For a totally baffling game which releases a lot of energy very quickly, try combining the two.

Divide the group into the four categories and position the four teams out of sight of each other.

When the whistle blows, cowboys have to shoot the Indians (by jabbing a finger in their stomach), Indians to tomahawk cowboys (by jabbing a finger in their back), cops arrest robbers (a hand clutching their shoulder), robbers cosh cops (a tap on the head). When someone is shot or arrested he or she immediately turns into whatever the attacker was (eg a shot Indian becomes a cowboy). After a few minutes nobody knows who anybody is any more, and so no one is sure who is going to attack them.

End the game before it gets boring by blowing a whistle. The winners are those who are back to their original roles when the whistle blows.

HIGHLAND GAMES

'It's a Knockout', which involves lots of silly and messy games within one programme, is a tired old idea. But, why not revive the formula by holding your own Highland Games?

With a little ingenuity, you can reproduce caber-tossing, shot-putting and sword-dancing. For example, get your sword-dancers dancing between crossed tent poles on a nine inch plank, suspended over a large tub of water!

Use your imagination: kilts, bagpipe music on tape, porridge-eating contests, haggis-identification tests (use a real tin of haggis from a delicatessen, a little Paxo stuffing, and some mince with flavouring, as the three alternatives).

If someone knows a bit about country dancing, get them to teach it to everyone. It's a bit like instant barn dancing, only funnier when it goes wrong!

TYPICALLY TROPICAL BAR-B

Encourage the young people to come to this social wearing Bermuda shorts and Hawaiian-style shirts—you could even hold a competition for the 'loudest' shirt.

Arrange for some summer sounds as background music (eg Beach boys tape or music from a steel band), during which you hold a limbo-dancing competition.

Other games could include a coconut shy, and 'pass the melon slice under the chin' team game. If you are able to hold this on a beach or by a swimming pool, all the better.

For some delicious bar-b food, what about sweet and savoury kebabs. For the sweet kebabs, skewer various fruits—pineapple, banana, grape, strawberry, etc, and for the savoury kebabs try fried steak, mushroom, onion and peppers.

SOUTH POLE SUMMER

This crazy social is a winter event for mid-summer. The venue should be a hill or grassy slope.

Insist the group come wearing at least wellies and a bobble hat (or balaclava) even if accompanied by shorts and T-Shirt. Then think up some winter sports and activities you can adapt for the summer. Here are a few to get you started:

Sledging Use very large margarine or ice cream containers, or something similar as moulds. Fill with water and freeze. You may find a sympathetic manager at a supermarket or freezer store will help to provide the large blocks of ice at a cheap price for you.

Use the large ice blocks to sit on and sled down the grass slopes. A cushion on the block may help. Supervise this game well, as it can become a little dangerous.

Snowball fight Supply large quantities of newspaper to two or more teams and give them ten minutes to make their snowball ammunition. Mark out a territory for each team. Then have a free-for-all for five minutes which you end by blowing hard on a whistle. The winning team has the least amount of snow on its territory.

Snowman competition Provide cardboard boxes, old footballs, carrots, white paint, hats, scarves etc. See which team can build the most realistic snowman.

Bonfire Conclude with songs around a fire, toasting marshmallows and drinking piping hot soup (even if it is 30 degrees centigrade!)

SANDWICH-MAKER

Divide your youth group/club into teams of three then send them off with a list of clues that will take them around to different homes near to the church. At each house the owner does three things:

1. Gives a short version of their testimony.
2. Gives any extra clues that you may want to introduce.
3. Gives the threesome one of the following things: two pieces of bread; lettuce leaf; margarine or butter sachet; knife (from church or your own cutlery); cheese slice; tomato.

The teams must gather one item from each stop and then find the 'health food inspector'. This is a leader in disguise situated near a location identified by the last clue. The teams must go up to whoever they think is the inspector and ask, 'May we eat our sandwich?' He or she checks that all the ingredients are there and gives it back to the team. Then to finish they must each take a bite from it!

EDUCATIONAL SCAVENGER HUNT

Most car rallies, scavenger hunts and the like are centred on trivial clues such as, 'How many windows are there in the launderette in the High Street?' But you can use this kind of competitive activity to teach important facts about the Bible.

Issue each team with a list of cryptic clues telling them where a series of message cards are hidden. When they work out the location of a message card, they read it and discover that it asks them a question about the specific area of teaching you want them to learn about. The cards offer various suggested answers, each of which bears a number. They note down the number of their choice and then they go on to the next clue.

When they have reached all the clues, they will have a series of digits making up a telephone number. If they ring this number, they can find out if they have won the prize, and what to do next.

The real value of this game comes in the debriefing afterwards: when you discuss which questions they got right and which they weren't sure about. It allows you informally to teach more about the subject and strengthen their knowledge of it in a painless way.

7
HALLOWE'EN
ALTERNATIVES

Many Christians believe that involvement in seemingly trivial Hallowe'en parties can feed an unhealthy interest in occult-linked activities. The apparent growth in interest among young people in the dark-side of the supernatural—including the use of ouija boards, tarot cards, etc—has resulted in many churches making a positive response to Hallowe'en.

Here is a selection of ideas for Hallowe'en alternatives with your youth group/club. They range from icebreaker games to teaching resources and activities to a full-blown event for you to use, adapt or get involved with.

CHIP SHOP SURVEY

To try this wacky alternative to 'trick or treat' you will need transport, some money to buy chips, soft drinks and a certificate to award to the best chip shop in town.

In cars or a minibus take your youth group/club to the six nearest chip shops to the church.

At each chip shop buy a portion of chips large enough for every member of the group to eat one or two chips. Explain to the person behind the counter that you are a church youth group/club out to sample the chips from every chip shop in the area.

After eating the chips go back to the cars or minibus and hand out reaction sheets for your young people to rank the chips on a scale of one to five on taste, colour, crispness, friendliness of the staff, value for money or any other categories you think are appropriate. Collect the sheets and clearly mark which shop the scores relate to.

Remember to take a couple of large bottles of soft drinks as eating salty chips makes for a mega-thirst!

Go round each chip shop in turn and at the end of the evening tot up the scores and return to the winning chip shop to tell them that the youngsters reckon theirs is the best chip shop in town. Present them with the certificate.

Take some photographs of the handover of the certificate and make sure you send a copy to your local newspapers along with a short press release about your youth groups' chip shop survey. A typical certificate could be worded thus:

Bloxwitch Town Chip Shop Survey

St Jude's Church Youth Club, having tasted the chips from every local chip shop, declares that _____
sells the tastiest chips in Bloxwitch.

A clip-art book will help you to design a good certificate, which should include a fancy border to give it an authentic look (check out the feature on clip-art on page 12 of *YOUTHWORK* magazine October/November 1992 for more info.)

Get the youth group members to sign the certificate before handing over to the chip shop owner. The local papers are likely to print such an unusual news story, especially if you supply them with a good quality black and white photo of the certificate handover.

It will be good publicity for the chip shop and for your youth group/club as well!

IT'S LIFE, JIM

'It's Life, Jim...But Not As We Know It' is the title of a 12-hour praise-rave party. The event is organised by the Shaftesbury Society, who publish a 'how to' manual with guidelines on how local organisers can put together the 8pm to 8am lock-in party.

As well as music, videos and games, a sponsored 'bop-till-you-drop' segment can raise funds for Shaftesbury's work with disabled young people, and the event can include disability awareness discussions, role-play and special 'disabling' games to help able-bodied teens experience what life is like for those who have a disability.

In many towns youth groups and clubs have joined together for inter-church all-night parties. To discover if there are 'It's Life, Jim' events being held in your area, or for details on running your own local party, phone the Shaftesbury Society on 081-542-5550.

DOORWAYS TO DANGER

This is the title of a twenty-five-minute video aimed at young people highlighting the dangers of getting involved with occult-linked activities. It is available from Sunrise Video Productions. Like all videos, make sure you watch it through first and read the accompanying helpful notes for leaders. These notes include ideas for discussion and Bible study on the subject of the occult.

A leaflet produced by the Evangelical Alliance accompanies the video. It draws on some of the stories and issues raised in the video as well as a more in-depth argument of why Hallowe'en has hidden dangers.

For copies of the video write to Sunrise Video Productions, 13 King Edward Avenue, Worthing, West Sussex BN14 8DB. Further copies of the EA leaflet are available from Evangelical Alliance, 186 Kennington Park Road, London SE11 4BT.

Another excellent resource worth investing in is Roger Ellis' book; *The Occult and Young People*, published by Kingsway and available from most Christian bookshops.

ST COLUMBA

Try this total participation play. You will need the following props: a boat (inflatable raft or upturned table); hairdryer(s) with extension leads; water pistols (or squeezy bottles); paper batons; small potatoes.

Divide the young people into four groups—the weather, the monks (including Columba), the Irish and the Scots.

Mark out Ireland and Scotland (with sea between) and read out the narrative slowly, emphasising the key words and pausing where appropriate to allow drama (and mayhem) to develop.

The group should act out the story as you read and do the following when you say these words:

Ireland: the Irish use potatoes to play catch with the monks.
Scotland: the Scots hit each others' legs with the paper batons.
Rain: water is squirted at the monks.
Wind: monks are set upon with hairdryers.
Columba: all shout 'Well, hurray!'
Monks: *gently* slap someone on the forehead.

Narrative

In the sixth century *Columba* and his *monks* lived in *Ireland*. After a dispute he had with the king,

93

men had been killed and now *Columba*, feeling very sad, wished to make amends. A hermit advised him to leave *Ireland* and take the gospel to the wild heathen Picts in *Scotland*. So he got into a small boat call a coracle, with his *monks*, and set sail from *Ireland*.The *rain* beat down on them and the *wind* blew against them as the *monk*s rowed towards *Scotland*.

'Farewell, *Ireland*; the *wind* and the *rain* won't stop us taking the gospel to *Scotland*,' said *Columba*.

Despite the bad weather they reached foreign soil, but because *Columba* could still see *Ireland*, he set off again in the coracle. More *rain*. More *wind*. Finally they landed on the little island of Iona, on the west coast of *Scotland*. They got out of the coracle and set about building a monastery, learning the language, growing crops, and attending the sick.

Before long, news reached *Ireland* that *Columba* and his monks were off building churches and taking the good news of Jesus, through the *wind* and the *rain*, to northern England, Iceland, the Faroes and of course all over *Scotland*. To this day the little island of Iona has always been special for Christians in Britain, as has the name of Saint *Columba*.

Follow-up

In groups discuss what life would have been like as one of the monks. What did they have to give up, and what difficulties were encountered? As a sixth-century monk, what would your strategy be for setting up a Christian community on Iona? What does living for Jesus cost us today? What would your strategy be today in your home for setting up a Christian community and reaching out to others from your base?

ALL SAINTS RELAY

Teams line up facing their own chair and table a few metres away. On each table is a cup, milk jug and teapot (use any suitable unbreakable receptacles). Alternate members of each team are Saints whose good deed it is to take their team-mates, the old ladies, to the cafe for a cuppa. A tinsel halo to rest on the Saint's head and an absorbent bib on the old lady are the minimum attire needed for the first couple in each team.

On the signal to start, the Saints must piggy-back the old lady to the chair and make her a drink, which she must finish before climbing back onto the Saint's back, who quickly returns to tag the next couple. They then dress up and the process is repeated until each couple in a team have completed. (Do not use hot drinks, Perhaps instead have water in the teapot and orange concentrate in the milk-jug.) Funny clothes to dress up in will enhance the game.

HIDDEN SECRETS

The word 'occult' basically means 'hidden' or 'secret'. It involves dabbling with forces we cannot see. People who practise these things are trying to 'tap in' to hidden powers. As an introduction to teaching on the occult, a wordsearch or puzzle based on a verse from the Bible about the occult and God's attitude towards it would reinforce the meaning of the word 'occult'.

8
CHRISTMAS CRACKERS

Here are eight great ideas and activities to adapt and use at Yuletide.

LYP-SYNCH CONTEST

Record beforehand on cassette some well-known Christmas songs, eg 'White Christmas', 'Jingle Bells', 'Ding, Dong Merrily on High', 'Merry Christmas' (by Slade), 'Silent Night'.

Contestants sing along with the tape, then you turn the sound down and the contestant sings on. The winner is the person who is still in tune and on time when you turn the sound back up on the cassette after a ten-second gap. Be prepared for some teeth-grating, ear-splitting renditions!

Give the winner a copy of the number one Christmas chart single.

ALL WRAPPED UP

Divide your group into teams of four. Supply each team with lots of super-cheapo Christmas wrapping paper, bows, ribbons and a roll of sellotape. Give all the teams three minutes to gift wrap one of their team in the wrapping paper. Award prizes to the teams with the best-wrapped team-mate, the most creative gift wrapping, etc. Play some suitable festive background music during this game.

NEW YEAR EXPECTATIONS

Hand out sheets of paper, envelopes and pens and ask each member of your youth group/club to write a letter listing their hopes and dreams for the coming year. When they finish, get them to put their letter into the envelope and address it to themselves. Collect up the letters and tell the group they will get them back at the last youth group meeting in December, when you can chat through the year and talk about what they did or didn't achieve and why.

SURPRISES ALL ROUND!

Give your minister or church leaders a pleasant surprise by suggesting the youth group delivers leaflets in the neighbourhood to promote the church's Christmas services. At the same time as delivering, your youngsters could sing carols. Watch out for surprised householders when you tell them you don't want their money, but instead invite them to church.

CHRISTMAS DOWN UNDER

Many Australians celebrate Christmas on the beach. Why not invite your youngsters to an Aussie-style Christmas party? Ask them to wear bermuda shorts and summer T-shirts. Make sure the venue is appropriately decorated with paper palm trees and that all the heaters are on full-blast, so that when everyone arrives they can strip to their beach wear.

Have a TV showing a videotaped episode from *Neighbours* or *Home and Away*. And if you serve food it should be barbecue-style with non-alcoholic cocktail drinks and ice-cold ice cream.

Play beach games like volleyball and boules or hold a hula-hoop or limbo contest.

HUMAN CHRISTMAS TREES

Split everyone into two teams and give them lots of Christmas tree decorations. The tallest lad in each team gets 'volunteered' to be a human Christmas tree. He holds out his arms for branches while everyone else tastefully decorates him with tinsel, hanging baubles etc. If you use Christmas lights take great care—electrocuting your tree could spoil the festive atmosphere! Video or photograph your Christmas trees for posterity.

THE ULTIMATE PRESENT

Hand out paper and pens and ask your youth group to imagine that Jesus was about to be born in their home town on 25th December, instead of Bethlehem 2000 years ago. Ask them to list three suitable presents that they would buy for the baby Jesus or his parents. Allow up to three minutes for thought.

Then read Matthew 2:1-12. Ask the group for their opinion on the choice of gifts for Jesus by the Wise Men. Explain that the gifts were both practical and symbolic—gold for a king and a valuable financial resource; frankincense (incense) for a priest; and myrrh (scented embalming fluid) for his burial.

THE BEST AND WORST OF CHRISTMAS

Hand out paper and pens and ask your group to make two lists: the things they like most, and the things they hate most, about Christmas Day. Allow a few minutes for this exercise and then get everyone to read out their lists.

Then ask them to make a third list of the laws they would pass to change Christmas if they were the Prime Minister. Suggestions could be ban the film *The Wizard of Oz*; put a 50% tax on alcohol bought to drink on Christmas Day; all mothers should have free loan of a dishwasher; outlaw the giving of socks, soap on a rope, bath salts, hankies or hand knitted jumpers as Christmas presents.

Finally, ask the group to agree a joint list of the things they think Jesus would most like to change about the way most people celebrate his birthday.

9
PARENTS' NIGHT

Making contact with and building relationships with the parents of the young people that attend your club is normally low on the priority list of most youth leaders and workers. That could be a big mistake. They can be valuable friends and allies.

Inform and involve parents of the young people that attend your youth group/club by inviting them to a special Parents' Night. (By 'parent' we mean all kinds: natural, step, foster and guardian).

As well as informing parents about the aims and objectives of the club, it also gives them a chance to meet you, ask you questions and find out about the content of the youth group/club programme in the term or year ahead. It is very worthwhile to establish good relations with parents. This is a great potential source of helpers, drivers and contributors.

NAME BINGO

As well as relaxing the parents, a few icebreaker games give them an idea of what their offspring get up to at the youth group/club, but do avoid the wilder, rougher games. Kick off with a scaled-up version of Name Bingo, the ideal mixer game. Give each parent a pen and a photocopied version of the card below. Parents mingle and get the boxes signed by someone who can claim the statement. Each box should have a different signature. Award a prize to the first to finish.

Enjoys playing Trivial Pursuit	Has two children older than 13	Belongs to a sports club
Never been to Spain	Has performed in amateur dramatics	Watches Eastenders
Has a green front door	Often shops in Tesco	Doesn't like pizza or burgers
Has a fish pond in garden	Lives in a bungalow	Drives a red car

VIDEO VIEW

Show a short video that was filmed at a previous youth group/club meeting. This should highlight some of the activities and typical programmes. Ensure there are some good shots of individuals for parents to spot! However, don't video a discussion or conversation likely to reveal confidences. The young people's permission should also be gained before filming begins.

Finish off with a short presentation of your plans for the youth group/club. Obtain feedback on your plans and ask if they have suggestions for future content or direction.

PREVIEW NIGHT

If you have planned your theme for the next term, why not provide a short presentation of your proposed programme. As well as overall themes you could provide snippets from a typical programme for the parents to take part in.

If you are using videos (eg *Lessons in Love*), show a short clip and encourage discussion over a cup of tea or coffee. Feelings and opinions may be strong if the topic is controversial. This may cause you some difficulties but if handled well will help you form relationships with parents and learn from them.

PARENT SUPPORT GROUP

Give responsibility to a small group of committed Christian parents for holding a meeting that takes place bi-monthly in one of their homes. They provide light refreshments and the youth leader provides the agenda. Include time to share ideas, receive feedback, pray for issues and concerns. Involve your church leaders where possible, but allow the parents to own this group, and hence feel more responsible for the youth group. Hear and use the advice and feedback that you are given. They can rotate which parents are in the support group, but keep the total number below twelve.

YOUTH GROUP SERVICE

A good way of getting uncommitted parents into church is for your youth group to take a church service in which they all contribute. If your term has had a theme, use it as the theme for the service. During the previous weeks take some time in your meetings to do things that can be used in the service—drama, sketchboard, songs, visual aids made by group members, testimonies. Involve the youngsters in all aspects of the service, whether it's welcoming people, taking the offering, operating the OHP and sound desk, or doing readings, but invite your minister to open and close the meeting. Print out invitations in advance for parents and consider a babysitting service using regular church members.

POST-SERVICE PUB QUIZ

Follow your youth group service with light refreshments and a pub-style quiz. Put parents and young people into teams and ask questions on a range of topics such as local history, chart music, film stars, Bible characters, current affairs, etc. Use multiple choice questions where possible with a mix of easy and hard, some geared for adults, some for teenagers.

YOUNG PEOPLE EXPLAINED

Many parents know little about the world-view, culture and pressures that affect their teenage children. You can help.

Music

Introduce parents to popular teen music with fun quizzes. These could include a quiz with small soundbites from songs which parents have to identify, or you could photocopy onto OHP acetate pages from *Smash Hits* which have song lyrics and read them through. Some parents may be shocked by the explicit sexual language many current love or rave songs contain.

TV, videos and films

Do a survey with your youth group about their viewing habits; how much TV, video, film they watch, favourite shows, etc. Show the results to parents along with a synopsis of the programme contents. Because so many teenagers watch their own TV in their own bedroom, many parents are oblivious to the watching habits of their children. Do the same with videos and films.

Peer pressure

Ask the parents to identify the peer pressures they felt when they were teenagers, then compare them to the intense pressures today's teens are under. Parents need to see how peer pressure has changed so that they can respond in relevant ways.

Put parents into groups and hand out some copies of teen magazines such as *Smash Hits, Just 17, Mizz* and *Viz* for them to browse through. Ask them to respond with general reactions and also specific comments about the advice pages. Were they surprised by the problems raised? How did they feel about the answers given by the agony aunt or uncle?

10
HIGH PROFILE EVENTS

High profile events are useful for building group attendance. A high quality event is easier to invite non-Christian friends to, and it can also build the confidence of the young people who attend the group—they can share in some of the reflected glory of belonging to a group or club which is able to arrange a good event. High profile events also help to kick-start a new term or launch a new club or group.

Such events can take a lot of planning, person-power and sometimes money, but done well they act as a shop window for the youth group or club and help build the profile of the church in the local community.

Here are four ideas for high-profile events that don't rely on the rather tired concert formula. Let them trigger off some of your own wild and wacky schemes!

MAC ATTACK

Book a room or section of the local fast-food restaurant and hold your youth group or club night there!

Many branches of MacDonalds and other fast-food restaurants have a separate dining area upstairs or in a side room. Find out from the manager how much it costs and the dates and times it is available. You should be able to get a group discount if you haggle! As well as burgers, pizza, french fries, etc organise a whole ninety-minute programme to make the evening special. You could book a band, hire a large screen video and show a movie, organise crowdbreakers—the sky's the limit.

In 1993, all across Canada, over a hundred youth groups booked pizza restaurants and got their young people to invite friends for food and an evangelistic presentation on large-screen video, transmitted simultaneously via satellite. It sounds crazy but thousands attended, many became Christians or wanted to know more and it raised the profile of the youth clubs who got involved.

Alternatively...

Another variation of Mac Attack is to invite the young people to attend in formal clothes—suits, shirts, ties, etc. Dim the lights, put candles on each table, and arrange for live music. The youth leaders should wear white shirts and black bow ties and act as waiters, taking orders and serving the tables.

A Big Mac will never be the same again!

FIREWORK PARTY

It took a lot of hard work and organisation, but one of the most successful high profile events I ever organised was an evangelistic fireworks party. Over twenty youth groups and clubs from the area attended, which helped cover the (considerable) costs.

Exciting but safe fireworks, hot food, an escapologist, crazy up-front crowdbreakers and a punchy ten-minute talk, all combined to make the evening highly memorable.

Display fireworks shouldn't be confused with garden fireworks. They are bigger, louder and more dramatic—but they don't come cheap. £200 is a realistic minimum figure for a fifteen-minute display. This means you will need to charge an entry price and invite other youth groups along to make sure the sums work. But don't be put off; organised carefully, this event will raise the profile of your youth work, increase attendance and attract potential new members.

Choosing a venue

Selecting the right site to hold a fireworks party is crucial. The ideal would be a large field at least the size of three football pitches, with good car parking facilities nearby, and a hall large enough for the expected attendance if the weather turns wet. The hall should also have a kitchen. Ideally the site will be on the edge of town so that there will not be a noise problem.

Setting a budget

Any sort of event of this size requires a simple but thought-out budget. This should be presented to and agreed by the church leaders and treasurer. List your expected income and expenditure with as much detail as possible. Be careful not to estimate too optimistic a ticket sales figure! See example.

Promotion

Phone the church youth leaders and workers in the district with as much notice as possible to let them know the event dates and details.

Alternatively you could make it an joint event, with other youth groups in the area taking a share in the financial risk and involvement.

Whichever option you choose, you will need to produce eye-catching promotional leaflets, handbills (A5), posters (A4 or A3) and tickets (sold before and at the gate). Tickets should be shown to gain admission and can be exchanged for the food (unless you plan to charge extra for this).

Sympathetic teachers can be approached to put posters up on school notice boards, local shops may put one up in a window. Handbills are a good

ST FREDA'S CHURCH YOUTH CLUB
FIREWORK PARTY BUDGET

INCOME: £
   Ticket sales—100 @ £2.50 each   250
   Subsidy from youth club budget   80
   Tuck shop sales   40
TOTAL   £370

EXPENDITURE:
   Fireworks   200
   Site hire   30
   Food: rolls, sausages, relish, napkin,
        squash, plastic cups   30
   Administration: photocopying handbills,
        posters, envelopes,
        stamps   12
   Safety equipment: cordon rope, safety
        goggles   10
   PA/lights hire   50
   Crowdbreaker games, props and prizes   5
   Tuck shop: soft drinks, crisps   33
TOTAL: £370

way to reinforce the details of time, place, cost and other details. Encourage youth group/club members to give them to friends—there is no substitute for word of mouth invites.

Safety

Every year people are seriously injured at firework parties, so make sure you do everything you can to prevent someone getting hurts. Many firework suppliers produce their own safety booklet and also sell copies of *Celebrate Safely*, a video which deals with aspects of display management. This video was produced by the Firework Makers Guild in conjunction with the Department of Consumer Affairs. Several companies including Bracknell Fireworks and Kimbolton Fireworks sell the video.

Spectators should be kept in a clearly marked roped off area, at least thirty metres away from the fireworks with their backs to the prevailing wind. Assign stewards in luminous jackets to keep spectators behind the ropes and to prevent anyone trying to set off a banger they brought with them (it happens!).

Two or three responsible adults should be in charge of letting off the fireworks. They should wear safety goggles, gloves, ear protectors and ideally a fire retardant boiler suit. They should rehearse carefully the order of firing and each must have a powerful torch.

Inform the police and, if it is a big display, the fire service and local authority environmental health officers at least a week beforehand, plus neighbouring landowners and anyone who may be upset by the noise, eg farmers, hospitals, old people's homes. Have a trained first-aider available at the event with a first aid kit. The local branch of the St John's Ambulance may be able to help.

If you have a bonfire ensure it is well away and downwind from the fireworks. It should be well supervised. Make sure it is completely extinguished before you leave the site.

Find out about insurance cover from your church secretary. You may find that the public liability cover for your church buildings will cover an event organised by the church—make sure you are covered. If not you will need to arrange special insurance cover. Some firework companies (including Pains) recommend a particular policy which includes cover for loss of revenue from cancellation of your display due to inclement weather.

Fireworks

Fifteen minutes of noisy, colourful fireworks are better than thirty minutes of weedy garden fireworks.

Fireworks should be set up in plenty of time. Examine them and follow the instructions carefully. Set pieces should be nailed to solid wooden stakes. Rockets, shells and mines should be tilted away from the spectators. Never angle fireworks over the heads of spectators. Ensure rockets fall onto open ground away from buildings, sheds or greenhouses. Beware of overhanging cables, trees, etc.

Whatever fireworks you order aim to finish the display with a good finale—a volley of shells or a big bang.

Programme content

Unless you spend a fortune the firework display will probably only last for fifteen minutes. You need to decide whether the total evening is to be spent outdoors (weather permitting), in which case you may need extra PA and lighting.

Outdoors or in you will probably want a magazine-style programme which could include: crowdbreaker games, a storyteller or preacher, interviews or testimonies, a band, etc. Close co-ordination with the cooking team is essential to ensure that hot dogs, drinks, etc are ready when required. Bear in mind that at least 15% of young people are likely to be vegetarian so ensure there is a bean or veggie burger alternative.

Wet weather contingency

Choose a venue with shelter so that if the worst happens people stay dry. Make sure the fireworks stay dry. Protect mortar tubes from distorting in damp earth by burying the tube in a large plastic bag.

Firework manufacturers and display organisers

There are over twenty companies in the UK who belong to the Firework Makers Guild. These include:

Astra Fireworks Ltd
Unit 5, Building 2
Sandwich Industrial Estate
Sandwich
Kent CT13 9LY.

Bracknell Fireworks Ltd
2 Bullbrook Row
Bracknell RG12 2NL.

Kimbolton Fireworks Ltd
7 High Street
Kimbolton
Huntingdon PE18 0HB.

Pains Fireworks Ltd
Romsey Road
Whiteparish
Wilts SP5 2SD.

Standard Fireworks Ltd
Standard Drive
Crosland Hill
Huddersfield HD4 7AD.

WORLD RECORD ATTEMPT

This idea works well in a school during lunchtime. Obviously you will need to get the school's permission first. It is a great 'taster' of what the youth club has to offer and a way to raise the club's profile.

Think of a crazy, gimmicky, world record that would require the involvement of a large number of people. Check to see if there is an entry in the *Guinness Book of Records*. If not, all the better. Put up posters, and have notices read out in assemblies that the world record attempt at tossing the biggest pancake, pulling the biggest cracker, eating the biggest sandwich or whatever, will take place on such a day and time.

I heard of one youth group that claimed a world record for the longest banana split in the world. It consisted of a (new and clean) length of plastic drainpipe cut down the middle, with bananas, scoops of ice cream, hundreds and thousands and syrup on top. Small plastic spoons were handed out and hundreds of pupils got down on their knees for a feast! Everyone also got an invitation to the youth club.

This sort of event will get the whole school talking. (If you want to get a listing in the *Guinness Book of Records* you will need to contact them first to find out what special requirements they may have.)

PARTY IN THE PARK

As the name suggests this event takes place at a park or common. When I helped organise one for my local church we hired a trailer from a lorry for a stage and used generators for power and PA. The programme was fast-moving—nothing took longer that ten minutes. There was no time to get bored and there were frequent moments when passers-by could be welcomed and gently drawn in.

The programme included taped music, competitions, messy crowdbreakers, drama, a joke contest, other audience participation games and a short punchy talk. The rolling magazine style kept attention and attracted passers-by.

We also hired an inflatable velcro-wall. These and other inflatables are fairly cheap to hire from local 'bouncy castle' operators. As well as being good fun they are a large visual magnet. One of the latest types is an inflatable boxing ring. Volunteers bounce around on the air filled 'ring' with huge soft padded gloves on their hands. It's like a glorified pillow fight and great fun to take part in or watch.

Add a barbecue sizzling away in one corner, a well motivated team of helpers and good weather and you have the perfect recipe for a high profile pre-evangelistic event.

But this kind of thing takes a lot of organisation and people power. Permission from the council, a lorry trailer or something similar for a stage, back-drop, PA, access to electricity or a powerful generator, stewards, counsellors, people to hand out flyers to attract passers-by, and a well-planned, slick, fast-moving programme are the basic essentials.

II
IS THERE LIFE BEYOND BLOXWICH?

Here are some ideas and activities to help your young people be more aware of the needs of people from other countries and cultures, and the work of missionaries sent out or sponsored by your church. There are also some practical projects for your youth group to get involved with to help make a difference in the life of a needy person.

BRAZILIAN NIGHT

Focus on one country and centre the whole theme of an evening or event around the customs, food, culture and language of that country—eg, Brazil. Contact the embassy of the country and explain what you are doing. Ask them for any information and posters they can send. If the country is a popular tourist destination, the local travel agent or the state airline may be able to help. Use the posters to decorate your venue along with drawn or painted flags of the country. If you can get hold of a tape of typical music from the country have it playing in the background as the young people arrive for the evening. You could serve some food specialities of the country concerned during the evening.

Try some of the following ideas, designed for a Brazilian night, but easily adaptable according to the country you have chosen.

Taboo

Play this version of the popular board game *Taboo*. One person takes a card and then gives verbal clues to get the rest to guess the word at the top of the card. However, the cardholder must not say any of the words on the card, if they do they are disqualified. Look over the cardholder's shoulder to make sure no 'taboo' words are used.

ORANGES
fruit
juice
pips
Jaffa

JUNGLE
forest
trees
plants
wood

FOOTBALL
soccer
Wembley
sport
game

Whoever correctly guesses the key word gets the next card to describe.

Prepare cards like the examples on page 130, which use words synonymous with Brazil, the largest orange producer in the world, famous for the Amazon jungle and for its footballers, including the legendary Pele.

Foreign 'Call My Bluff'

Play this popular TV game but using Portuguese words (the main language in Brazil). Ask for six volunteers, three on each team. In turn each team is given a word in Portuguese (find them in a phrase book from the library). They have to decide which of three definitions the opposing team give is the correct one. Hand out three cards to the opposing team. One has the correct definition, the other two are blank except for the word 'bluff'—they quickly have to think up a convincing definition.

Loudest Bermuda

Ask everyone to come dressed in loud Bermuda-type shirts. Offer a prize for the most garish!

Limbo dancing

Hold a limbo dancing competition. Play suitable carnival or steel band music in the background.

In the news

For several weeks in advance, look out for and keep newspaper stories about the country you are focusing on. Use these as background information or to trigger a discussion on the issues and problems affecting the country.

If Brazil, it could be a story about the country's big debt to Western banks, or the plight of the street children, or about the rapid destruction of the Brazilian rain forest.

SPONSOR A CHILD

World Vision is one of several charities through whom individuals or groups of people can sponsor children to help with the cost of their education.

Making contact with and offering practical assistance to a person can be a very effective way of focusing understanding and interest in a country. However, this should not be undertaken lightly. A commitment should be for more than just a year. The children involved may have been rejected in various ways already in their young lives. Try not to add to this by dropping them after the minimum sponsorship time.

MEET THE MISSIONARY

If your church missionary is home on furlough invite him or her for a quick-fire question and answer session with the young people. Suggested questions: weirdest thing you ate; the thing you missed most from the UK; your favourite chocolate bar; your biggest problem; the best thing about the local people; why go abroad to serve God? How can we support you and pray for you best?

When the missionary is back abroad, get the young people to write letters or send cassette messages, photos, magazines, small luxuries including their favourite chocolate bar (which you remembered from the answer to the question above).

The South American Missionary Society (SAMS) produce *Centre Point*, a twice-yearly youth group resource with meeting ideas 'to excite and enthuse your youth group about mission.' For more information contact Malcolm Ingham, SAMS, Allen Gardiner House, Pembury Road, Tunbridge Wells, Kent TN2 3QU.

THIRD TRACK

Tear Fund produce *3rd Track*, an excellent resource which focuses on the culture, problems, and opportunities of the two-thirds world. A sixteen page mini-magazine, it contains meeting ideas, poems, quizzes, discussion starters, fact files, etc. It is available free from Tear Fund, 100 Church Road, Teddington, Middlesex TW11 8QE.

ADOPT A GRAN

Build contact with an old peoples' home or individual old people in or outside the church. The social services department of your council should be able to suggest people who would value the contact and help which your young people could provide. Practical jobs like digging the garden, washing windows etc, will be appreciated, as will help at a day care centre. However, make sure your young people are accompanied. Some youth groups have held a service at an old peoples' home. A mixture of well-known old hymns, a short Bible reading and a brief testimony or prayer will go down well.

THIRD WORLD MEAL

Tell your young people not to eat just before next week's youth club/group as you will be serving a meal.

As the young people arrive give them a dice: if they throw a one or a two they get to eat the whole meal you are about to serve; if they throw a three or a four they get bread, a small lump of cheese and water; a five or a six means they get nothing.

Be strict—don't allow the 'have nots' to share the food of the 'haves', as this will ruin the point you are trying to make. Sitting down together around a table where some eat well, some poorly and some not at all will provoke some outrage and a great discussion on world famine and the inequality between rich and poor nations.

WORLD VISION 24 HOUR FAMINE

Once a year this charity organises a twenty-four-hour fast to focus attention on the needs of the poor and to raise money for their work to alleviate famine. For further details contact World Vision, Dychurch House, 8 Abington Street, Northampton NN1 2AJ.

CHRISTMAS CRACKER PROJECT

Since 1989 millions of pounds have been raised for Third World relief and development projects by Christian young people who have got involved in Christmas Cracker. This has happened through innovative 'Eat Less—Pay More' restaurants and 'Tune In—Pay Out' Radio Cracker stations, and most recently 'Aid and Trade' Christmas Cracker-terias.

During December local church youth clubs/ groups run Crackerterias in High street shops or church halls, serving and selling fairly traded tea and coffee.

Contact the Christmas Cracker office to find out more details of this project which has attracted widespread national media attention. Write to: Christmas Cracker, Cornerstone House, 5 Ethel Street, Birmingham B2 4BG.

Christmas Cracker is a joint project of the Oasis Trust and ALPHA magazine. The *Christmas Cracker Manual*, which gives lots of help and ideas, is published by Kingsway.

12
STARTS AND STOPS

First impressions are important, and yet so often a youth group meeting has a patchy start. This is because the leaders don't want to begin until everyone has arrived. In practice this means those who arrive early or on time hang about waiting until the latecomers arrive. Week by week the start time gets pushed back as people arrive later and later in order to avoid hanging around in a half-empty room or hall.

Avoid an empty, awkward atmosphere by having some background music playing from the moment the doors open. Choose the music carefully. It needs to be popular with the majority of young people who attend (you'll never please everyone), but also acceptable to the ethos of the church. Choose upbeat music that will convey a feeling of excitement, not slow ballads or love songs more appropriate to a restaurant atmosphere.

Some games and activities can be used from the moment the first youngsters arrive, which will occupy their minds, integrate them with other group members as they arrive, and loosely link into or introduce the theme that week.

Put together a wordsearch worksheet. Hand out the wordsearch and a pencil as young people arrive. Use words that relate to the theme of the week. Latecomers will have less time to solve the puzzle, thus rewarding those who arrived on time.

A wide variety of picture and/or word games can be used which link well into many themes. Before young people arrive blu-tack or Sellotape onto the walls and furniture of the room or hall the clue cards. Each card will have one picture or one written question and a number. As the young people arrive hand out paper and a pen and explain they need to move round the room writing down the identity of each numbered picture or answer to each numbered question.

Some 'round the room' game examples follow. Again, the latecomer is penalised with less time to complete the game. Do not extend the game to give the latecomer time. This will encourage punctuality and make your life easier!

STARGAZING

To introduce a theme of heroes or fame, stick pictures of well-known sports, film, TV and music stars onto paper. Use newspapers, magazines, TV listings, etc as the source for the pictures.

SELLING FAST

To kick off an evening on the theme of the power of the media, or materialism try this: Cut out adverts from glossy magazines, making sure you omit the product brand name. Use some obscure ads as well as the more famous ones.

TRUE OR FALSE

Write multiple choice or true-or-false questions, one on each card around the room. This can be adapted to work with virtually any theme or topic; eg money—the currency of Portugal is the lire (false); drugs—people who use cannabis are more likely to use other drugs (true).

RECORDBREAKERS

The *Guinness Book of Records* is a great quiz source for a whole range of games ideas. To link in with the theme of the church as the Body of Christ, select true or false questions based on amazing records to do with the human body (tallest, fattest, most births, oldest living, etc); to link with creation, green issues or the end of the world, check out the section on the living planet for amazing facts and figures to do with the earth.

DINGBATS

Use the board game of the same name for the
questions or make up your own dingbats on cards
and put them round the room. For example:

$$\frac{\text{MAN}}{\text{BOARD}} = \text{man overboard}$$

ALL MIXED UP

A series of anagrams, written onto card makes a
good opener. Link the anagrams into the evening's theme. If the theme is 'music' use names of
pop stars and musicians, eg OHEN NOTJL =
ELTON JOHN.

GOO-GOO-GOO

Arrange for all the leaders and young people to bring along a picture of themselves when they were a baby. Matching the baby to the person is always a good chuckle. Baby 'bathtime' shots are especially good fun!

NAME THAT SONG

Written lyrics from well-known songs is yet another 'round the room' option. Again, with a little work you can choose appropriate songs to link into a large range of meeting themes.

THE GOOD OLDE DAYS

If you want to underline the historicity of an event recorded in the Bible kick off with this intro game. Select pictures or photographs from different historical events and periods. The young people have to write down a year in which they think the event occured. Twenty points if they answer spot-on, one point less for each year they missed by. So if someone wrote down 1950 for a picture of the coronation of the Queen they would get 17 points (20 minus 3, as the answer is 1953).

VALUATION

Use this intro game to link the theme of values, materialism or debt. Use pictures of a wide variety of goods cut out from a catalogue. The one who can come closest to the correct value of the item wins a point. The winner is the one who accumulates the most points.

CRISP TASTING

Buy at least eight different flavoured crisps. Before the young people arrive empty each packet into a bowl which is labelled with a number one to eight. Keep a careful record of which flavour goes into which bowl. As the young people arrive give them each a paper and pen and ask them to taste and record which flavour each bowl contains. Make sure you buy a few of the more unusual flavours, as well as the more popular salt and vinegar and cheese and onion flavour.

Give the winners a packet of plain ready-salted crisps as a prize.

END ACTIVITIES

How you end a session is just as important as how you start—if not more.

Reflective games and activities that allow for and encourage discussion and one-on-one talks are helpful.

Serve drinks—from low-key coffee or coke to a full-blown non-alcoholic cocktail bar. Sipping a drink is conducive to conversation rather than a quick exit. Often the most significant conversations will occur after the 'official' programme has ended.

Asking for help to clear up at the end of a session also allows for youngsters to chat with you, but beware of being left alone with one young person after everyone has gone. You leave yourself wide open to accusations of abuse.

Asking for a reaction to the youth club in general or the programme on that particular evening can get young people to open up and be honest. You may learn some surprising facts about what the young people do and don't like if you stop and ask.

To make this feedback creative why not hire or borrow a video camera to record their comments, then play them back next week. Or if not a video why not record their views on a dictaphone or portable tape recorder. Another variation is a questionnaire. Or why not ask the young people to write a short letter to themselves about what they have learned that week. Put the letter in an addressed but unsealed envelope. Then during the week put into the envelope programme details or a special event promotions flier, seal the envelope and send it off in the post to arrive before club next week.

13
BOOKS FOR IDEAS

Ten years ago you could probably count the number of ideas books on Christian youth work on the fingers of one hand. Since then a virtual explosion of new books, including many from the United States, has left the youth worker or leader almost spoilt for choice. To help you make an intelligent decision when buying I have listed the titles I am aware of with a brief descriptive note. But whatever books you use—including this one—don't forget my advice in the opening chapter to adapt the ideas for your own particular group of young people.

A Really Great Assembly by Grahame Knox and Chris Chesterton (Scripture Union). Two veteran schools workers provide the reader with over 30 assembly ideas, easily adapted for youth club epilogue talks.

All Together Forever by Phil Moon (CPAS). This 10-session booklet is based on Ephesians and designed for use with thirteen to eighteen-year-old Christians.

Each session includes warm-ups, discussion starters, creative ways to read the Bible, prayer formats and ready-to-copy worksheets.

Assembly Line by Andrew Smith (CPAS). Assembly talks easily adapted into youth club talks.

Assembly Point by Grahame Knox (Scripture Union). Secondary school assembly ideas which also make good five to ten-minute talks.

Beginnings by various authors (Bible Society). A series of eight Bible-based studies which includes the excellent *Just Looking* used and adapted by many churches for adult as well as young enquirers about the Christian faith. Booklets include warm-up exercises to relax the group, discussion questions and a leader's guide.

Big Ideas for Small Youth Groups by Patrick Angier and Nick Aiken (Marshall Pickering). This collection of icebreaker games and whole meeting ideas was designed with the smaller youth group in mind and includes some excellent and original ideas along with a few old favourites.

Boredom Busters by Cindy S. Hansen (Group/Scripture Press). A collection of 84 low and no-cost activities designed to inject fresh life into a flagging meeting.

Creative Ideas for Youth Evangelism edited by Nick Aiken (Marshall Pickering). An excellent compilation of tried and tested ideas to help your youth group grow.

Creative Programming Ideas for Junior High Minis-

try by Steve Dickie and Darrell Pearson (Zondervan/ Youth Specialties). A range of meeting ideas, games, music, drama and theme nights. This does not rank as one of the better American ideas books for younger teens.

Crowdbreakers by Bob Moffett (Marshall Pickering). Excellent introductory chapters on the appropriate use of games, plus a good selection of icebreaker games. First published in 1983 *Crowdbreakers* is deservedly one of the best-selling ideas books ever.

Crowdbreakers 2 by Bob & Gilly Moffett (Marshall Pickering). Some good games, but like most sequels not as good as the original!

Far Out Ideas for Youth Groups by Wayne Rice and Mike Yaconelli (Zondervan/Youth Specialties). Despite the naff title and cover there are plenty of usable games and drama skits.

Family Party Games by Pip Wilson (Marshall Pickering). A good range of games suitable for all ages with plenty of golden oldies.

Fun Old Testament Bible Studies by Mike Gillespie (Group/Scripture Press). The 32 meeting outlines make this an impressive adapt-and-use resource. Each session includes a photocopiable worksheet or graphic.

Get Away by Arlo Reichter (Bible Society). If you are planning a residential break or holiday for your youth club/group this is *the* book to get. As well as helpful practical advice and safety tips there are a range of theme ideas for your weekend or longer.

Get 'em Talking by Mike Yaconelli and Scott Koenigsaecker (Zondervan/Youth Specialties). Over 100 excellent discussion starters plus some useful sections on encouraging discussion and interaction.

Great Ideas for Small Youth Groups by Wayne Rice (Zondervan/Youth Specialties). An excellent selection of games, all designed to work well with a smaller than average youth group.

Group's Active Bible Curriculum Series by various authors (Group/Scripture Press). Two series of topic-based booklets; one for eleven to fourteen-year-olds; one aimed at older teens. Each booklet follows one theme which is broken up into four meeting plans. Well-produced worksheets come with permission to photocopy, plus games and discussion ideas.

Homemade Youth Retreats by Robert Doolittle (St Mary's Press). Written for Catholic youth groups, the ideas for residential breaks translate well across the denominations.

Hot Talks by Duffy Robbins (Zondervan/Youth Specialties). The 25 talks printed in full, including jokes and illustrations, will be of limited use to UK youthworkers, although the introductory chapter on how to give a talk contains some useful guidelines.

It's Tuesday Night Again by Mary-Ruth Marshall (JBCE/Quest). As well as a wide range of ideas and 36 complete meeting plans, this book offers help in planning, leading and evaluating a youth work programme.

Jigsaw edited by Jim Belben (Bible Society). A series of booklets which look at each form of writing in the Bible: the Law, Old Testament History, Poetry and Wisdom, Prophets, Gospels, and New Testament letters. Designed as a small group workbook for older teens and students who are keen to improve their Bible knowledge. Includes creative group interaction ideas.

Journeys of Discovery by Lance Pierson (Small Group Resources). A 6-session study guide for new Christians—overflowing with creative ideas and approaches.

Junior High Game Nights by Dan McCollam and Keith Betts (Zondervan/Youth Specialties). Zany games ideas for younger teens which link into 12 major theme nights. Many of the ideas are highly memorable and include a concluding talk slot outline.

Junior Youthbuilders by Patrick Angier (Marshall Pickering). A mix of meeting outlines, projects, socials, art and craft activities, talks, games, worksheets and quizzes aimed at eleven to fourteen-year-olds. Many of the ideas are not particularly new, but as a collection of ideas for use with younger teens it's a useful resource.

Know Ideas! edited by Phil Moon (CPAS). Subtitled 'Serious fun for youth groups' this no-frills manual offers icebreakers, Bible study outlines and whole-session activities aimed at 'Christianised' young people.

Launchpad by various authors (Scripture Union).

An excellent variety of icebreakers, discussion starters, sketches, photocopiable sheets, poems, games, stories, video and music suggestions aimed at eleven to thirteen-year-olds. Not a loose assortment, it is impressively focused to bring out the clear teaching of scripture.

Power Pack by Bob Moffett (Scripture Union). Meeting plans first published a decade or more ago in *Buzz* magazine (the forerunner of *Alpha*).

Power Pack 2 by Bob Moffett (Scripture Union). More of the above.

Power Lines by Bob Moffett (Scripture Union). Yet more of the above.

Quick Crowdbreakers and Games for Youth Groups by various authors (Group/Scripture Press). A good range of relay games, pair games, games for teams and non-competitive activities for the whole group.

Quick Skits and Discussion Starters by Chuck Bolte and Paul McClusker (Group/Scripture Press). Despite some heavyweight Americanisms these 18 short dialogues and monologues, many of them amusing, will promote discussion. Not sketches—more role plays—they require virtually no rehearsal or line learning. Topics include family relationships, dating and peer pressure.

Quick Studies by various authors (David C. Cook). This major series of ready-to-use meetings covers the whole New Testament chapter-by-chapter in six volumes. Each study contains a summary of the Bible chapter, a crowdbreaker or opening activity, a discussion starter to highlight the main points and a 'wrap-up' application.

Serendipity Youth Bible Studies by Lyman Coleman and Denny Ryberg (Scripture Union). An excellent series of workbooks chock-full of invaluable and easily-adapted Bible study outlines and worksheets.

New Serendipity Youth Bible Studies by Terry Dunnell, Andrew Graystone and Chris Powell (Scripture Union). Six study booklets each containing six complete meeting plans including Bible study, multiple choice questions, discussion starters and games ideas. Comes with a leader's guide.

Serendipity Youth Ministry Resource Book by Lyman Coleman (Scripture Union). A good selection of games and interactive Bible studies for Christian teenagers. Includes some particularly good group building exercises and studies with multiple choice non-threatening options to questions.

Simulation Games by Pat Baker and Mary-Ruth Marshall (JBCE/Quest). A combination of role-play and board games on a variety of themes. The quality of this Australian book is variable—some ideas are great, many are ordinary, a few are truly desperate!

Spectacular Stinking 'Rolling Magazine' Book by Pip Wilson (Marshall Pickering). The paperback version of Pip's crazy 'Rolling Magazine' show from Greenbelt. A creative mix of activities, icebreakers, discussion starters and audience-pulling 'up front' messy games involving custard, eggs, grapes, etc, combined with Pip's non-competitive philosophy.

Spectrum Music-Based Curriculum by various

authors/artists (David C. Cook). Each one of the Spectrum range includes a cassette tape of Christian music accompanied by discussion questions, activities and Bible studies on issues raised by the songs. A creative idea but quite dependent on a knowledge of the musical artist.

Super Ideas for Youth Groups by Mike Yaconelli and Wayne Rice (Zondervan/Youth Specialties). More wacky games ideas from our American cousins. Despite the cringe-worthy title and cover design this is one of the best ideas books from across the pond.

Talksheets by David Lynn (Zondervan/Youth Specialties). A range of meeting ideas in three separate books for Junior High (young teens), Senior High (older teens) and parents. The sequels: *More* (Junior, Senior, Parents) *Talksheets* maintain the excellent standard of these ready-to-use outlines plus photocopiable worksheets.

Teaching the Bible Creatively by Bill McNabb and Stephen Mabry (Zondervan/Youth Specialties). Excellent ideas to improve the quality and creativity of Bible studies, improving your teaching technique and motivating young people into studying scripture themselves.

Teaching the Bible to Children by Tony Castle (Marshall Pickering). Activity based learning programmes for eight to twelve-year-olds designed to open the Bible for this age group. A good range of games, exercises, memory aids, talk outlines and suggested songs.

Teen Discussion Guide by various authors (Rainbow). Scenarios based on various dilemmas offer the young people a choice. The decision they make leads to a further discussion starter and provides an unusual level of options and personal control. Be warned—the Americanisms need adapting.

Tension Getters by Mike Yaconelli and David Lynn (Bible Society). A compilation of the best from two American books of the same name this book will provide plenty of excellent discussion starters—almost indispensable!

The Christian Youth Manual by Steve Chalke (Kingsway). This 'how to' manual on the basics of running a youth group/club includes some helpful programming ideas along with theory, pastoral advice and skills training. If you're starting out in youth ministry this is a got-to-have book!

The World Christian by Robin Thompson (Lynx). An excellent workbook for older teens or students on world mission and cross-cultural communication. It benefits from excellent layout and graphics which make the weighty contents more accessible.

Theme Games by Lesley Pinchbeck (Scripture Union). Vintage playground games and party classics adapted and linked, sometimes tenuously, with one or more of 200 Christian topics.

Topic Books edited by David Day and Linda Smith (Lion). A range of booklets designed for use in the secondary school classroom as part of a Personal and Social Development course or Religious Studies lessons. The topics covered in the series include:

anger, heroes, growing up, the environment, work and death. Plenty to take and adapt in these well-crafted books.

What Will We Do On Friday Night? by Glen Smyth (JBCE/Quest). Over 100 ideas from Australian youth leaders. Good games ideas, weak Bible studies and discussion starters.

Young People and the Bible by Phil Moon (Marshall Pickering). Highlights include some creative meeting outlines, photocopiable worksheets and the conviction the author brings to the subject of teaching scriptural principles to young people.

Youthbuilders by Nick Aiken and Patrick Angier (Marshall Pickering). An excellent collection of old and new games, meeting ideas, social events, art and craft activities and a chapter on programme planning and organising a weekend away.

Yoyo by various authors (Scripture Union). Four-part series of ready-to-use meeting programmes, discussion starters, Bible studies, activities, talks and games. An excellent and highly flexible resource.

10-minute Devotions for Youth Groups by J.B. Collingsworth (Group/Scripture Press). Over 50 rapid-fire punchy talk ideas that would work best with enthusiastic youngsters who are likely to contribute freely.

52 Ideas For Secondary Classroom Assemblies by Janet King (Monarch). Designed for school assemblies, these excellent outlines are just as good in a youth club setting if you are looking for a punchy, memorable talk.